# TIME WITH GOD

# TIME WITH GOD

## GRAHAM CLAYDON

TIME WITH GOD
Copyright © 1979 by Graham Claydon

First published in 1979 by Inter-Varsity Press
38 De Montroft Street, Leicester LE1 7GP, England

First Zondervan printing  June 1982

**Library of Congress Cataloging in Publication Data**

Claydon, Graham.
   Time with God.

   Originally published: Leicester, England : Inter-
Varsity Press, 1979.
   Bibliography: p.
   1.   Spiritual life.      2.   Prayer.      I.   Title
BV4501.2.C557   1979              248.3           82-7033
ISBN 0-310-45202-3                               AACR2

Scripture references are from *The Holy Bible, New International Version*. Copyright © 1978 by New York International Bible Society.



*Printed in the United States of America*

# Contents

# Prologue

You have set the scene.
Your new Bible lies open
as your mouth opens to pray
and the thought comes
uninvited
into your mind,
"What exactly is going on here?"

This is the subject of this booklet.

# TIME
# WITH
# GOD

# 1

# Setting God at the Center

**Drinking**

"The more emotion one invests in them [possessions] the more chances of significant gratification are lost—the more committed to them one becomes the more deprived one feels like a thirsty man drinking salt water."[1]

"Whoever drinks the water I give him will never thirst. Indeed, the water I give him will become in him a spring of water welling up to eternal life" (John 4:14).

This booklet could be said to be about drinking. For obvious reasons such a statement is not reproduced on the cover, being wide open to misunderstanding! Yet it is a striking, even refreshing picture of how our spiritual thirst is quenched. Like all analogies it is inadequate, its chief drawback being that God is personal while water is mineral. We never relate to water; we simply use and enjoy it. Only by relating to God, however, are we satisfied. Furthermore, we dare not presume simply to use or even enjoy Him just for our own benefit. Indeed should we try to do so He would almost certainly withdraw a consciousness of His presence until we regain our perspective as to who He is and who we are.

The Creator, our Lord, however loving and personal, is not at our beck and call. The amazing fact is that He invites us to come to Him at all. Not surprisingly He invites us on His own terms. To our eternal surprise and joy, when we do come to Him, we find that we will be satisfied in time and in eternity.

Whether we use contemporary sociological jargon like "investing emotions" or timeless images like "thirst" we all know the experiences they describe. We desire a great closeness to others without which we are restless and dissatisfied. More than this, as Christians, we have come to realize that we need a closeness to God our Creator without which we are incomplete and unfulfilled. In fact, it has been this realization that has led us to faith in Jesus Christ through whose life, death, and resurrection we are able to come into a close relationship with God.

Nevertheless many of us would have to admit that we are vague, lazy, and ill-disciplined in our development of this relationship. For, like other relationships, our friendship with God needs time and energy to be developed.

Jesus promises us an "inner spring" of satisfaction which is His picture for His own presence within us through His Spirit. Just as physical thirst is quenched by ordinary water so spiritual thirst is satisfied by the gift of the Holy Spirit. When we become Christians we receive the Spirit and experience spiritual satisfaction. It is our relationship with our God that satisfies, and because God fails neither in quality nor in availability we need never thirst again, just as Jesus promised.

In practice we often find ourselves to be "thirsty" Christians; either because we are failing to drink or because God is stretching our capacity for Himself and we need to drink more deeply. In either case we need consciously to draw into ourselves more of the spiritual life that flows freely from God our Father through the Spirit.

## Relating

"Blessed are those who love you O God and love their friends in you and their enemies for your sake. They alone will never lose those who are near to them for they love them in one who is never lost, God our God."[2]

"People can only love outside and can only kiss outside but Mr God can love you right inside and Mr God can kiss you right inside."[3]

As we press on exploring our experience of God we now need to move beyond the water analogy to another Bible picture; that of the Father-child relationship. It is not surprising that many of Jesus' contemporaries found His teaching about this relationship hard to swallow. No man had ever dared to refer to God as his heavenly Father, let alone had the audacity to invite others to do the same. Certainly their incredulity seems a more reasonable response than the bored familiarity some Christians appear to display in their prayers, as though it is no great privilege that they can address God as "Father." But even worse than this is the heretical and patronizing idea that God was lonely and made you and me to brighten up His mundane existence. The very fact that these false concepts are so widely held drives us to examine the heart of our relationship with God.

"God is love" (1 John 4:8). He is love in Himself. As Father, Son and Spirit He is always sharing within Himself.

Each person of the Trinity loves and satisfies the others. Such a self-sufficient God of love is never lonely nor in need. Creation, then, is an expression and overflow of that love. We are made, in God's image, to share in that love which is already full and complete in God. And we are satisfied deeply only as we consciously relate to God, who is love.

"God is love" and the heart of love is giving. The Father shares with the Son and the Spirit, the Son shares with the Father and the Spirit who, in turn, shares with them both. We see a glimpse of this eternal character of God as we watch Jesus communicating with His Father throughout His days on earth.

Observe Him spontaneously breaking out into conversation with His heavenly *Abba* ("dad"):

"I praise you, Father, Lord of heaven and earth, because you have hidden these things from the wise and learned, and revealed them to little children" (Matt. 11:25).

In the joy of seeing His Father's principles unfold and in delight at communicating that awareness to His Father, Jesus bursts into prayer. Or see Him struggle beneath the olive trees' twisted trunks in moonlit Gethsemane:

"Father . . . not my will . . . but yours be done" (Luke 22:42). Here it is the struggle, pain, and agony of His dilemma that Jesus expresses in prayer.

These are man-sized windows through which we can begin to understand the mutual exchange of thought and feeling that exists in the heart of God.

"Is church sex?" six-year-old Anna asked her counselor. He questioned her quizzically before concluding, "I got the idea she was trying to put across. All the universe has got a sex-like quality about it. It is seminal and productive at the same time. The seeds of words produce ideas. The seeds of ideas produce goodness knows what!" Anna had grasped, in a flash of childlike insight, that God, who is love, has created a universe of giving and receiving, offering and taking, interchange and exchange.

Now, fascinating though it may be, what has all this to do with our personal relationship with God pursued in prayer and study of the Bible, for this is the subject of this booklet? In the first place it has to do with our awareness of the God we relate to. A stunted awareness of God can but lead to a stunted relationship with Him. Indeed, without a deep concept of the God we love and aim to serve the danger is that prayer and Bible study will degenerate into mere religious ritual. In the second place, and naturally following on from this point, we need to see our relationship with God as the culmination of creation. That phrase is meant to impress. God has expressed His love in creation. In particular He has demonstrated it in creating us in His own image. And He has gone further than this by entering even more deeply into human experience, in Jesus, so that we might enter more deeply into a relationship with Him again in Jesus.

Our personal experience of this relationship begins with an act of faith or trust in Jesus. This was combined with a deep recognition of our own lostness caused by our moral disobedience and guilt. This repentance, together with personal faith in Jesus and His act of reconciliation on the cross, are the foundation stones of Christian experience. But every fresh stepping stone forward with God is also a fresh, deeper act of repentance and a deeper, fuller expression of our faith in the risen Jesus.

### Sharing

"As my blood systematically, to the pump's rhythm pumped into Kitty's veins, bringing life visibly to her face, my blood pouring into her to keep her alive, my life reinforcing hers, for the first time I truly understood what love meant."[4]

"And God, do look after yourself, for if anything happens to you we're done for."[5]

I have purposely not explained all the quotations in detail but these do demand some comment. Both point to our depending on God not only for our physical existence but also for our spiritual life.

The former quotation in particular dramatizes the fact that the heart of love is a deep sharing of everything we have and are. In creation God has shared Himself with us. In human history, by becoming man, He has gone ever further in sharing. And that act of sharing became the deepest exchange of love ever to take place when Christ was crucified. On the cross the just died for the unjust, the innocent became guilty so that we might be declared innocent and be justified.

When we become Christians we consciously enter into this great exchange that Jesus called the New Covenant. We acknowledge our guilt and receive forgiveness. We offer ourselves to God and receive the Spirit of Christ. The Spirit brings to our life a new capacity to respond to God and a new desire to do so. This is the foundation of our spiritual experience.

We build on this foundation by continuing our experience of sharing with our God. This is where prayer and Bible study and meditation come into their own, for they are no mere appendages to Christian living, nor optional extras for the Christian who wants to go places fast. They are the practical roots of our continued experience of relating to God.

They are not all there is to that relationship but they are the gateway to it.[6] God has chosen to channel His voice to us through the Bible. We are invited to channel our response to Him through our prayers. Both prayers and the Bible will take us into areas of communication with God beyond themselves but they remain God's chosen pathway to these further areas. Through the Bible God speaks to us. Through prayer we speak to God. These are the foundations of our loving exchange with Him.

[1]P. Slater, *The Pursuit of Loneliness* (Pelican, 1970).

[2]Augustine, *Confessions* (Penguin edition, 1961).

[3]Fynn, *Mister God, This Is Anna* (Collins, 1974).

[4]Malcolm Muggeridge, *Chronicles of Wasted Time* (Fontana, 1972).

[5]Anonymous small boy.

[6]This booklet does not cover any of the apsects of our corporate Christian experience, i.e., holy communion, church services, prayer meetings, group Bible study, etc.

# 2

# The Bible

### Listening

The film *Papillon* ends with Henry Charrière flinging himself into the sea, spreadeagled on a raft of coconut-stuffed sacks. He drifts away, possibly into the sunset, but I'm not sure of that! The book of this true-life escape goes further and records his experiences bobbing around at sea as the mainland finally appears:

"It is in the midst of the elements of nature—the vastness of the ocean, the never ending waves; the tremendous green roof of the forest—that one feels so infinitely small in comparison with everything around; and it is perhaps then that without looking for him one finds God . . . he is to be found in the wind, the sea, the sun, the jungle and even in the fishes that he must have scattered with so free a hand that man might be fed."[1]

Charrière does not mean the same as the Bible does by "finding" God. He means becoming aware that God is: Scripture means coming into a personal relationship with God. Yet Scripture includes creation as one of the most basic ways God speaks to us, as we read in Psalm 19, for example,

"The heavens declare the glory of God;
    the skies proclaim the work of his hands.
Day after day they pour forth speech;
    night after night they display knowledge.
There is no speech or language
    where their voice is not heard.
Their voice goes out into all the earth,
    their words to the end of the world."

This particular poem goes on to speak of a further way God has spoken to all men, through conscience. Each of us has some sense of moral law and the rightness of goodness. Thus God speaks to us through this awareness before we recognize this as the voice of God. Yet when God so speaks we are left without knowing Him. This is in fact the situation of mere "religion," man's attempt to understand and approach God. What is seen of God in nature and moral law becomes a good and right religion as far as it goes. But it cannot go far enough. It cannot restore our lost relationship with God and bring us into personal communication with Him. This is why Jesus is the way, the truth, and the life.

Nevertheless, before Jesus was on earth, God spoke even more personally than through creation and conscience. He spoke through the Jewish prophets. He defined and applied His law far more personally. He made His character far more clear. He shared His desire to love and relate to His people. But even this revelation was still incomplete and comparatively ineffective because men's hearts were spiritually dead and noncommunicative. So God spoke again, unmistakably.

"In the past God spoke to our forefathers through the prophets at many times and in various ways, but in these last days he has spoken to us by his Son" (Heb. 1:1—2).

Before this God had spoken through men, now He spoke as man. All that He wished to share with us He now spoke directly through human lips and with human vocal chords. There was now no mistaking His will or His way for us. Jesus Christ was God speaking directly.

It is unfortunate that no matter how clearly we may speak there is no guarantee that someone else will understand. Communication is as much a matter of listening as telling. God has also seen to this problem. When we become Christians we receive the Spirit of Christ from God and He clarifies our thinking and enables us to respond to what we hear.

"God has revealed it to us by his Spirit" wrote Paul (1 Cor. 2:10). He did not mean what some Christians have seemed to imply, that the Spirit gave a secret interpretation of the message of God. Rather he meant that the Spirit enables us to take in and respond to the true meaning of God's words as given by Jesus and recorded in the New Testament.

The recording of God's Word was of course a key stage in establishing communication between God and man; the message of the prophets and special spokesmen of the Old Testament for the first part of the Bible; the words of Jesus and His message recorded by the people He authorized to write it, for the second part, the New Testament. The Spirit of God directed and safeguarded the recording of the whole Bible. So when we have a Bible before us we have the key to responding to our Creator. Having a key, however, is not the same as letting ourselves in. How do we get into the Bible?

The answer to this question is both spiritual and practical. Spiritually we need to ask God by His Spirit to open our inward eyes to see what the Bible is really saying. Martin Luther records how this first happened to him:

> "I beat importunately upon Paul . . . most ardently desiring to know what St Paul wanted. At last by the mercy of God, meditating day and night . . . I began to understand . . . I felt that I was altogether born again and had entered paradise itself through open gates. There a totally other face of the entire Scripture showed itself to me."[2]

There is all the difference in the world between reading the Bible as an academic studying for an exam and a child of God anxious to hear Father's voice. It is this difference of approach that the Holy Spirit suddenly gave Luther and the same Spirit will give us a spiritual understanding of Scripture if we ask Him.

## Framework for learning

This section will bring a sigh of relief from some readers: at last some straightforward words on practical experience! And my first practical comment is very direct. Read the Bible often. If that comment needs further explanation then I would add, strive to read the Bible daily.

Every morning when we read the paper or listen to the news a certain perspective on life forms in our minds. Often it is pessimistic, uncertain, and frustrating. The Bible is God's antidote to our limited world perspective. It turns us back to see life from God's eternal viewpoint, not our own shortsighted one nor the chaotic view of the media. Not that the Bible is escapist. It is as full of murder, rape, war, and disaster as any newspaper. Yet it is able to put even this within an eternal perspective. This is the attitude of mind and heart in which we need to approach each day. Not all the Bible is equally designed to give us God's total picture on things. Yet almost every page of it will thrust us back to see life through God's eyes and not our own.

Beyond this general refocusing that daily Bible reading gives us I would like to suggest a simple framework of thinking that we can bring to it. It is, I believe, one that is given by Scripture itself and not an artificial imposition on God's Word. Essentially it is a framework of response to reading the Bible. Here it is:

1. Praise and thanksgiving
2. Repentance and confession
3. Obedience and guidance.

*1. Praise and thanksgiving*

One misconception that needs to be dealt with before we will freely praise God is a sneaking feeling that God should not need our praise and that it is somewhat conceited of Him to demand it. What this misconception completely ignores is that praise and thanksgiving are a delight and joy to us just as much as they are to God. In fact, it is a mark of man's spiritual blindness that he does not see any point in praising and worshiping his Creator. It's easier to stare at the TV set, or even do a little extra work, than to enjoy praising God.

Even as Christians it's hard for us to praise and give ourselves to the joy of praise as the Jews managed to in the Old Testament times. A constant refrain of theirs was:

"Give thanks to the LORD, for he is good" (Ps. 107:1). Not surprisingly Paul urges Christians to do even better: "Be joyful always . . . give thanks in all circumstances" (1 Thess. 5:16, 18).

Once we see just how much God has done and how great He really is, such an attitude will become natural and not forced. As we read Scripture we will be renewed constantly in a vision of God and His activity which will stir our praise and thanks. At least five things will leap out at us as we submit to the thinking of the Bible; five ideas that will always move us to give thanks.

1. God. He is good, He is love, He is great, He is truth, He is fruitful, merciful, pure and strong. He is . . . read for yourself and find out. Then give thanks.
2. Creation. All of us are moved deeply at some stage in our lives by natural beauty. Maybe a sunset or a view or some tiny bird or insect may release our sense of wonder.

   "For since the creation of the world, God's invisible qualities—his eternal power and divine nature—have been clearly seen" (Rom. 1:20).

   Scripture encourages us to see God in everything that is good, beautiful, and wonderful.

   And seeing God we are urged to praise Him. Before long this praise sinks deeply into our lives giving us new strength and joy. While daily newspapers may drive us increasingly to despair, daily Bible reading will teach us to rejoice.

3.  Rescue. The Bible is a history of rescue. In the Old Testament God's people were constantly being rescued from political, economic, and spiritual oppression and so learning to praise Him. It is particularly important in reading the Old Testament to look for this theme of rescue and to identify with it. The reason we can identify is that as Christian people we have been rescued from the greatest oppression of all, that of sin and spiritual death. This is the central theme of the New Testament and indeed of the whole Bible. Thus, as we read it, we are taught to praise God constantly for His rescuing us through the life, death, and resurrection of Jesus.

4.  Personal. Because the Bible is historical it teaches us to look for meaning and significance in our own daily lives. It educates us to look for God at work. Then when we do begin dimly to see what He is doing in us and around us we again have much to thank Him for.

5.  People. "I thank my God every time I remember you" wrote Paul to the Philippians. Scripture teaches us about this new attitude to people. Not only do we learn to see all men as made in the image of God but we particularly see Christians as our brothers and sisters in God's new family. The more we go on as Christians the more deep relationships we make within that family. People then become a growing source of joy to us and a constant impetus to praise.

*2. Repentance and confession*

Not only does Scripture introduce us to God as He really is but it also faces us with ourselves as we truly are. We are compelled to recognize how far short of God's goodness we have fallen and continue to fall. The Bible shows us this in various ways.

1.  In specific statements about what is right. Sometimes these are obvious, as in a clear statement like the Ten Commandments. At other times they are less direct. Thus when we read Paul's command to be joyful it may suddenly dawn on us how much we complain and grumble in the course of the average day.
2.  In examples of failure. Apart from Jesus, every character in Scripture failed somehow at some time. Thus every person we read about points us to our own failure at some time in some way. Like David, suddenly made aware of his sin, we will respond "I know my transgressions; my sin is always before me" (Ps. 51:3).
3.  In examples of faith and trust. As we read about the faith of Abraham or the commitment of Paul, who wanted only to know Christ, share His suffering and experience His power (Phil. 3:10), we will increasingly face our own unbelief and lack of dedication. This would be unbearably depressing were it not for the offer of God's forgiveness and His working in us. "But with you there is forgiveness; therefore you are feared" (Ps. 130:4).

God is revealed as a forgiving God to those who acknowledge their sin and accept His cleansing. This is the whole basis of Christianity. Through God's own self-sacrifice in Jesus Christ's death there is new life, new hope, a new beginning. In Christ we go on leaning on God's promised forgiveness:

"If we confess our sins, . . . he will forgive us our sins" (1 John 1:9).

Only when we see our faults do we hunger and thirst for righteousness. But when we do that God promises we will be satisfied by seeing progress through His Spirit and work in our lives.

"Blessed are those who hunger and thirst for righteousness; for they will be filled" (Matt. 5:6).

Perhaps I should explain this rash of quotations. In one sense it seems obvious. If I am going to eulogize about the power of the Bible to transform our daily attitudes and experience then the best way to do so is to let it speak freely for itself. Furthermore these quotations could be a help in getting down to some Bible study with the question "What do I read?" Start discovering the Bible by finding and examining these verses.

### 3. Obedience and guidance

Having learned to accept and worship God and to return to Him through His rescuing us in Jesus then we need to know how to live to please Him. How does loving God affect our approach to work, our family, sex, marriage, money, ambition, holidays, reading, study, music, etc.?

In fact, the Bible has plenty to say on all these subjects—and others! Often its directives are clear. More often there is room for our own decisions to be made based on biblical principles. A biblical attitude to money, for example, will be built up from Old Testament laws and the wise sayings of the Book of Proverbs clarified by the teaching of Jesus and expressed in an actual Christian workaday situation in various New Testament letters.

At other times Scripture will be more concerned to transform our attitudes than to give us clear outward directives. A Christian lifestyle could be said to be the result of the transformed character that the Holy Spirit produces, as depicted in Galatians 5:22–23.

When it comes to the more personal and specific matters of guidance the Bible helps us by being a constant stimulus to our faith. The God who has so faithfully guided His people in the nitty-gritty of life, from Abraham onward, will securely guide us in our daily decisions and actions. How He does so is very much a matter of experience, but in the Bible we find the principles to work on and the encouragement to keep trusting Him.

This framework, then, keeps us asking, or better praying, the right questions as we approach the Bible. Namely what should I be praising You for, God? What should I be confessing and seeking strength and moral courage for? What are You saying to me about my daily lifestyle, relationships, use of time, money, and energy? You will notice how this means we shift from the Bible to prayer all in one breath, as it were, just as in a conversation we move from listening to talking and back again to listening without any very conscious change of approach. There is, however, much more to say about prayer, so first let me tackle some further practicalities about Bible reading. It will, I think, help to list them fairly boldly and discuss them briefly.

### Practicalities

*1. Versions*

There are many translations of the Bible from the original Hebrew and Greek. On the whole each new translation makes some improvements on the previous ones and the latest translations are more likely to be contemporary in language and phraseology. Of the recent translations the most successful seem to be:

1. *The Revised Standard Version:* An accurate translation sticking close to the word pattern as well as the meaning of the original languages. As a result it can be stilted to read.

2. *The Good News Bible* (Today's English Version): It has a fully contemporary ring about it. It aims to elucidate the meaning rather than parallel the actual structure of the original languages. A most readable translation, though sometimes missing the finer theological nuances.

3. *The Jerusalem Bible:* A Roman Catholic translation which is a fresh and pleasing reading.

4. *The New International Version:* This is the version I am quoting from throughout this booklet. It is a freer, more contemporary version of the RSV.

If you plan to take Bible reading seriously spend some time choosing your version; buy a cloth bound book because it will last longer.

## 2. Starting

The Bible is not a novel or even a fully consecutive history book. Thus it does not lend itself to being read nonstop from Genesis to Revelation. In a sense it starts in the middle, or more strictly two-thirds through, for in the Gospels God is fully revealed in human history. Jesus makes sense both of the Old Testament and the future as pictured in Revelation. It is therefore important to grasp Jesus before anything else. Much of the Old Testament is relevant to us only indirectly. Thus its principles are valid but they are often worked out in ignorance of later principles that God revealed to His people, or in cultural situations that no longer exist. To start in a book like Leviticus, without any explanation or help from other Christians, may lead to confusion.

Many people find it helpful to start with a Gospel (like John) and some letters (like Philippians or James) and get the feel of Bible study. And remember the framework already discussed earlier. Some have found it helpful to use a system of marking their Bible to begin to apply this

26

framework. Thus promises of God could be underlined in red, commands in green, and prayers circled in pencil, etc. It's probably much more exciting to invent your own system.

I hope you have already discovered that systems like these, which trick the mind into remembering things, are very helpful for exam purposes! But the stakes for running well as a Christian are far greater even than those involved in doing well in exams.

### 3. Aids

There are a number of books and booklets designed to facilitate effective Bible reading. Each has its place and its usefulness at various stages of our growth as Christians. One may be more helpful to some than to others but the list on pages 43–44 can give you some ideas. New aids are constantly emerging and the list will soon grow out of date. Nevertheless some guidance is better than none.

There are also a variety of notes around for daily Bible reading which can be helpful although inclined to be superficial. Try them and see!

### 4. Notebook

Perhaps I might be permitted to mention this topic in a personal way. Before I took God seriously I kept a diary. On reading it now I frequently find it boring and obnoxiously self-centered. Later I kept a notebook of occasional jottings whenever God seemed to teach me something new and relevant. This record—a jumble of Bible verses, quotes, prayers, and thoughts—I consider one of my most valuable possessions for it enshrines something of how God has mercifully dealt with me as an individual over a number of years. Perhaps my comments will encourage you to do the same—or maybe put you off the idea completely!

[1]Henri Charrière, *Papillon* (Pan, 1971).
[2]Ed. John Dillenberger, *Martin Luther. Selections From His Writings* (Anchor, 1961).

# 3

# Prayer

"It can turn one alternately to laughter and tears to find people fully admitting the need to set several hours aside daily to master shorthand or a foreign language, and blandly assuming that they can conquer sin and know God by a few sleepy moments at the end of the day."[1]

Prayer is not easy. Although it comes naturally to us once we know God, there remains an effort to get down to prayer that seems to stay with us all our lives. The explanation for this is twofold. First, as Christians we retain our fallen humanity as well as receive a new spiritual nature. And there is nothing that our fallen humanity objects to quite so much as prayer. Second, Scripture warns us that there is a devil, a spiritual being opposing God's work. And there is no greater target for his opposition than prayer. Just as an army can be destroyed if its lines of communication can be cut off so a Christian can be reduced to a state of total ineffectiveness if the devil can stop him from praying.

Thus Jesus teaches that prayer is a definite act of the will. It means choosing a time, finding a place where we can be quiet and concentrate, and actually going there and blocking off the outside world as much as is in our power. In fact, I would recommend looking up Matthew 6 where Jesus speaks about prayer. Verses 5 and 6 speak of the need for these deliberate acts of the will:

"When you pray"
"go into your room"
"close the door"
"and pray."

Each of those directives involves a further decision to get going. Not only does Jesus stress this necessity to steel ourselves to pray but the Christian's experience confirms His teaching, as we would expect. Note these quotes from a book by a preacher named P. T. Forsyth:

"To learn to pray with freedom force yourself to pray."

"Pray till you are in the spirit. Do not say, 'I cannot pray until I am in the spirit.'"

"Compel yourself to meet your God as you would meet your promises, your obligations, your fellow men."[2]

It is the last of these quotes that has given rise to the title of this booklet. Once we see the issue it is only logical that we should be as organized and definite in spending time with God as we are with any human whom we love.

Oddly enough, the need for us to be organized and to make time to be with God can be obscured by a genuine awareness that God is always with us. We can pray anywhere, anyplace, anytime. Our relationship is not dependent on being alone in peace and quiet. All this is wonderfully true. What it forgets, however, is that this abiding relationship must be kept fresh and personal by a definite time of openness and directness with God. In ordinary human relationships friends need times when they can sit down and "catch up" as well as sharing life together. Jesus not only taught the need for a specific "when-you-pray" time but He also demonstrated it by going off to pray frequently Himself, away from everyone else. It seems that He had a favorite prayer place on the slopes of the Mount of Olives (Luke 22:39).

I intend to return to some thoughts on the when and where of our prayer times in a concluding practical section. Meanwhile I hope to have made a good case for a definite, committed approach to times of prayer—time with God.

**Framework for praying**

"Lord, teach us to pray" (Luke 11:1).

It is good to establish the need to meet regularly with God in a time of prayer but what do we pray about? It was apparently just this dilemma that faced Jesus' disciples and led them to ask this question. It is fortunate for us they did ask it because now we have Jesus' specific answer to their request. The answer came in the shape of a model prayer, one that could no doubt be used as such but one also that gave a pattern on which to base our times of prayer.

*1. Talk to God about Himself.*

"Father"

Does it matter how we address God? Although the Bible gives us many ways to address Him it encourages us as Christians to call Him Father. For this word evokes a sense of security and trust, of love and respect in a way that no other title for God can. Just coming into God's presence in prayer, being aware of Him and calling Him "Father" begins a change in us. Such prayer is like tuning up or tuning in: it brings us back to God's wavelength and into harmony with Him. When we call God "Father" we remind ourselves that we can speak to Him about anything and He will understand. True prayer should begin with telling God how we feel about Him and how we are in general. Even if honesty compels us to admit how bad we feel right away, it should not deter us from coming. And if we are indignant with God there is biblical precedent for telling Him just that. The psalmist did and the prophet Jeremiah had a number of complaints to bring to God; so did Job. Even our pains and complaints we bring to our Father. Prayer begins with freshly accepting and acknowledging the heart of our relationship with God who has made us His children through our commitment in faith to Jesus Christ.

*2. Talk to God about other people.*

"Hallowed be your name, your kingdom come."

Having responded to God ourselves we are now taught to pray for others to respond to Him. In one way we are also continuing to pray for ourselves; that we may honor Him and that His kingdom might advance in us and through us. But we move beyond ourselves to others that they too might aim to please God and live with Him as their king. At heart this involves praying for the conversion of others. Such prayer is obviously valid, for Jesus taught it: it is also complex.

"In any petitionary prayer for people three personal beings are involved and what happens as a result will emerge from the interplay of all of them."[3]

Petitionary prayer is no penny-in-the-slot affair: it involves complex spiritual laws. It involves the interplay between the will of God, our own wills, and the wills of those for whom we are praying. Scripture also hints that the angelic powers behind creation are involved in a spiritual struggle in which our prayers play a significant part (see Dan. 10:12–13). So Jesus encourages us to pray for others to make Him king and this we should do whenever we pray. We should also pray for Christians everywhere who are involved in the task of proclaiming Him as king. Because of the enormity of this responsibility we need to break it down into manageable segments. Our concern must be for the whole world but in practice we do best to begin with the world we actually know and experience day by day. We should pray for our families, roommates, friends around us. It's good to develop a concern for missionaries, evangelists, and Christian workers we hear about. Most important though, we should pray for those we know and relate to most closely. It is good to pray for political and social problems as well as spiritual (1 Tim.

2:1–2) but always our concern should be that men and women might do what is right and pleasing to God even if they do not honor Him as such.

*3. Talk to God about your needs.*

"Give us each day our daily bread."

Only now does Jesus permit us to turn to the sort of things that most people rush into when they pray . . . "Lord I need . . . ." We are taught that God is concerned with our deepest practical needs, but all too easily these needs become barriers between us and God. Our only concern with God is that He meet our wants. Jesus teaches us to see our wants in their proper context, following on God being honored and loved in the world. In fact, where God is loved our needs are going to be more fully met. Where there is justice and concern, love and care, people are going to share, the hungry will be fed, the sick cared for, and the lonely befriended.

So there is strict logic behind the pattern of prayer we are given here. Once we have gained this right outlook, however, we should not be afraid to pray for practical needs; for food and jobs and homes and finance. God's provision may come through others, through our own efforts or through a redirection of our desires, but in some way or another He will give us our daily needs.

*4. Talk to God about forgiveness.*

"Forgive us our sins for we also forgive everyone who sins against us."

Many of us find this request jars at this point because we have already prayed about forgiveness in our first approach to God as our Father. Perhaps we should be prepared to surrender even our instinctive responses to the pattern Jesus gave us. Or more likely should we not take a fresh look at ourselves, having prayed for our needs? Who are we to ask God for anything? Selfish, critical, insensitive to others, how can we expect to go on receiving God's love and approval and care? Yet we do so! Does not this drive us to reassess our relationships with others in the light of God's mercy to us? And such a reassessment will inevitably bring a new sin to light with a fresh challenge to forgive and love and understand others even as God forgives, loves, and understands us. So we need constantly to bring all our relationships with all their joys and agonies consciously to God so that we can both receive forgiveness from Him and receive the ability to forgive others as we do so.

*5. Talk to God about your weakness.*

"And lead us not into temptation."

We are weak and in ourselves lack the resources to resist evil. Unless God keeps us inwardly and guards us outwardly from overwhelming circumstances we do not stand a chance against evil. Jesus teaches us to turn this recognition into daily prayer for God's inward grace and outward protection. We would be well advised to take Him seriously or we will find ourselves in trouble before we realize it.

### Summary

It would be a help at this stage to couple the responses we picked out from Bible reading with this analysis of the prayer Jesus gave us. Perhaps this summary will provide a practical pattern for the time we spend regularly with God.

*1. Talk to God about Himself and your relationship with Him.*

> Praise Him for Himself
>> His creation
>> His salvation
>> your experience of Him
>> your Christian friends.

*2. Talk to God about others.*

1. That individuals will make Jesus king, that is, become Christians.
2. That you will be able to help people to become Christians.
3. For those involved in the work of the kingdom in this way (missionaries, ministers).
4. For Christians to uphold the values of God's kingdom.
5. For men in authority to uphold those values even when they do not acknowledge God.

*3. Talk to God about your needs.*

*4. Talk to God about your relationships.*

*5. Talk to God about your weaknesses and need of His help.*

As Christians we should be inspired constantly to pray by both the example and teaching of Jesus. Added to these we can draw strength and stimulus from the example and experience of Christians who have put Jesus' teaching into practice. So I close this section on prayer with a stimulating quote from a sermon on the Lord's Prayer by one of the church fathers, Gregory of Nyssa.

"The effect of prayer is union with God and if someone is with God, he is separated from the enemy. Through prayer we guard our chastity, control our temper and rid ourselves of vanity. It makes us forget injuries, overcomes envy, defeats injustice and makes amends for sin. Through prayer we obtain physical well-being, a happy home and a strong, well-ordered society. Prayer is the seal of virginity and a pledge of faithfulness in marriage. It will refresh you when weary and comfort you when sorrowful. Prayer is the delight of the joyful as well as the solace of the

[1]W.
[2]P. T. Fors
[3]J. A. Baker, _The
Todd, 1970).

# 4

# Appointment With God

Most of us would agree that if we left our studies or football practice or visits home until the times we "felt like it" then life would become disorganized to the point of being chaotic. Everything worthwhile needs planing and organizing. It is not that we necessarily do not enjoy any of these things, although there may at times be an element of this in our failure to plan. More often it is simply the effort of getting around to things that holds us back. Once we recognize this simple fact it will become obvious that we will need to organize a regular time with God. An appointment with Him needs to find a place in our daily timetable.

### Where to pray

I have a theory that is very romantic and not very realistic. It is that we are all designed to respond most naturally to God at sunrise and sunset! Perhaps it is just the memory of vacation experiences of doing just that which has created my romanticism. There is, nevertheless, an element of reason in this theory, as well as reflections of it in Scripture (Ps. 5:3 and Gen. 3:8). The element of reason is that it seems sensible to start the day as we mean to continue it, consciously in fellowship with God. And as the stillness of evening quiets our hearts it somehow creates that sense of reflection on the day that is most conducive to sharing our hearts with God. Having said this I admit I seldom see the sunrise nor do I often notice the sunset behind the office building of central London! This is a stark reminder that we have to work out the practical realities of our walk with God in the reality of twentieth-century urban life. A few of us may be fortunate enough to escape the main thrust of these pressures, but not many. In particular the structure of

our daily working lives, even with the comparative freedom of being students, will necessarily dictate some of the
limits of times we may choose to spend with God. At the
risk of stating the obvious I have ventured to list the various
times that most of us can choose for such an appointment,
together with some comments about their suitability.

1.  In the morning, either before or after breakfast. In
    theory we should be fresh. You may not be.
2.  Last thing at night. Only choose then if you are hon-
    estly alert and awake.
3.  Alternatives are the lunch hour, or earlier in the eve-
    ning before you are too tired. (If you choose one of
    these, still get into the habit of beginning the day
    with a conscious prayer of commitment to God.
    Maybe use a devotional book such as *Daily Light* to
    form your thoughts on a few verses from Scripture,
    even if your main Bible study is later.)
4.  If you have a long train or bus ride alone to work then
    use this time for God. Some people find that a walk is
    ideal for praying; a walk to work is an ideal time to
    pray.
5.  If you choose lunch time the problem is where to go.
    A quiet corner in a restaurant or lunch room, a park,
    or a church could be suitable.
6.  Similarly if your living situation is noisy and over-
    crowded the problem will be where to go to be quiet
    with God. The bathroom is all right until someone
    else wants to get in! Better look for a quiet place on
    campus or a park or church—even a public library if
    it is near.

Obviously our timetables and situations change
throughout life. Babies, for example, upset the routines of
the most disciplined people. So it's good to experiment and
have a variety of approaches.

## Aids to prayer

Continuing to be practical about our appointment with God let me say a word about aids to prayer as I did about aids to Bible reading.

### 1. *A hymn or chorus book*

Martin Luther said, "When I cannot pray I sing," a piece of advice I have interpreted by playing hymns on the piano. If you play a guitar there is even more flexibility for music to play its part in your time with God. Incidentally, it may help to add a comment of John Bunyan: "God who made the nightingale also made the crow"!

### 2. *Books of prayers and meditations*

Sometimes when we feel dry or listless, using other people's words can warm our hearts and snap us back into an awareness of God that frees us again to pray. There are great Chrsitian classics along these lines like á Kempis' *Imitation of Christ*. Then there are the liturgies of the church designed to help us worship. Also we will come across a constant flow of contemporary meditations, prayers, songs, and poems that we can look out for and use in our times with God as we find them useful. Some people may feel all such aids are barriers to true prayer and they are quite entitled to their opinion, even though I do not hold it.

### 3. *Lists*

When it comes to prayer for God's kingdom to come we may well feel that we cannot carry sufficient information in our heads and in our hearts. Some would respond by saying that unless the things we pray for spring naturally to mind then we cannot be concerned enough for them to pray for them. Others, perhaps more conscious that the spirit may be willing but that the flesh is weak, emphasize the need for a notebook to remind us of people and situations to pray for. Into this book we can slip letters and photographs, maps and prayer letters all of which will trigger off our memories and facilitate our intercession. The more we undertake to pray for, the more necessary some sort of system may seem. Some people pray for different things each day in order to cover as many people and situations as possible in a week.

## 4. *Meditation*

The main danger of being too organized over our time with God is that a good and positive routine of prayer and Bible study ends up by boxing up God into His set appointment time. And during this time we are so busy answering questions from our Bible reading or speaking earnestly to God that we do not give ourselves time to be deeply spoken to by God nor even time just to enjoy a sense of His presence.

Francis de Sales once said, "Some people are nearer to God in their sleep than others are when they pray." I think that he meant that prayer that is simply us telling God about what we think and feel does not give His Spirit any room to guide us or change our thinking. On the other hand a constant inner attitude of openness to God, beginning in our times of set fellowship with Him, means that He can constantly work in us, even when we are asleep.

It may be stating the obvious, but I am presuming it has already been realized that prayer is not necessarily speaking out loud to God. It is not even necessarily "speaking" words at all, even in our minds. It is more like direct thought transference to God, if you like. In the same way God, of course, speaks to us not only directly through words of the Bible but also through the thoughts He transfers to us as we think about Him. You will notice that Jesus checked every idea of God held by the people of His day against the written authority of the Scriptures. Any ideas we may gain about God, whether from books or people or our own minds, must similarly be checked against the written authority of Scripture. Scripture is God's check on our private thoughts to ensure that they are true to His thoughts and are not a projection of our own ideas. The parallel danger to wish-fulfillment in prayer is sinking into daydreams that cease to be directed toward God. The borderline between meditation and daydreaming can be very slender!

Praying out loud is a safeguard against daydreaming. It also compels us to think through what we really do want to say to God. Praying silently but in words is similarly effective for doing this, except that it is easier to forget what we are trying to say. For this reason prayer with words, vocal or mental, is always important in our fellowship with God.

More important than this kind of prayer however is the more meditative type of prayer in which we may imagine things or people or situations and then lift them to God as we do so. Going over a situation we have been through, before God, can help us see our feelings and how we could do better in the future. Running through a talk we have to give, or a situation we have to face, as we are in prayer with God is also a valid form of meditative prayer. Worship can sometimes consist of imagining something beautiful and feeling praise to God. It can of course be actually contemplating beauty and praising Him. For most of us prayer will become a mixture of vocal, mental, and meditative communication. A right balance of these will help us keep disciplined but not rigid. I add a quote on the subject of meditation that has helped me keep the balance in this area:

"True prayer must also proceed from profound reflection upon our own lives as well as from the study of God's word. For God desires to speak to us not only through Scripture but also through our experience of life. Meditation is the spiritual act whereby the Word . . . prayer and our experience of life are united in order that they may mutually penetrate the soul as a whole"[1]

That concluding statement reminds us again to see prayer and the Word, the Bible, as the means whereby we are more and more deeply penetrated by God until, by His grace, we are eventually "filled to the measure of all the fullness of God" (Eph. 3:19).

## 5. Extra times of prayer

This closely follows the last section since such extra times with God may well involve more meditation. At certain times in our lives we will face major decisions about the future that we sense need much guidance from God. At other times we may feel that in spite of our routine times with God we are losing steam spiritually. These are the times to plan longer, openended times with God. Some Saturday go on a retreat for the morning and spend the time with God. One vacation, go off into the mountains armed with books and pour out your heart in prayer. Spend time looking back on all God has done for you and then look ahead in detailed prayer to all you long for Him to do. Some people recommend fasting in connection with such extra times of prayer. Jesus certainly suggested this (Matt. 6). Even missing one meal occasionally can give an hour to spend extra time with God.

What better way to conclude a booklet about our own prayer than with one of Paul's regular prayers for others as he spent time with his God:

"This is my prayer: that your love may abound more and more in knowledge and depth of insight, so that you may be able to discern what is best" (Phil. 1:9—10).

[1]Emil Brunner, *The Divine Imperative* (Fontana, 1970, under the title *Love and Marriage*).

# Suggestions for Further Reading

## Aids to Bible Study

Select verses for daily devotions:
   (Useful for starting the day in a hurry or under exam-pressure!)
J. Sidlow Baxter, *Awake My Heart* (Zondervan)
Oswald Chambers, *Daily Thoughts for Disciples* (Zondervan)
Andrew Murray, *God's Best Secrets* (Zondervan)
F. B. Meyer, *Our Daily Walk* (Zondervan)
*Daily Light* (Zondervan)

Bible study:
Gordon Fee and Douglas Stuart, *How to Read the Bible for All Its Worth* (Zondervan)
Herbert Lockyer, *All About Bible Study* (Zondervan)
Lawrence Richards, *Creative Bible Study* (Zondervan)
Howard Vos, *Effective Bible Study* (Zondervan)
*Search the Scriptures* (InterVarsity Press)

Commentaries:
Good News Commentaries (Falcon/Collins)
The Bible Speaks Today series (InterVarsity Press)
Tyndale New Testament Commentary series (InterVarsity Press)
Bible Study Commentary series (Zondervan)

General introduction to the Bible:
John R. W. Stott, *Understanding the Bible* (Zondervan)
Graham Claydon, *The Bible Is for You* (Falcon)
Robert Lee, *The Outlined Bible* (Zondervan)

## Helpful books on prayer

Brother Lawrence, *The Practice of the Presence of God* (Baker)

Thomas á Kempis, *Imitation of Christ* (many publishers)

Andrew Murray, *Waiting on God* (Moody)

Andrew Murray, *The Inner Life* (Zondervan)

Hope MacDonald, *Discovering How to Pray* (Zondervan)

Richard DeHaan, *Pray: God Is Listening* (Zondervan)

O. Hallesby, *Prayer* (Augsburg)